OUR STAND

By Tim Damianidis

This eBook was published in 2023 by

M. Damianidis

First Edition

DIGITAL ISBN-13: 978-0-6455221-7-4
PAPERBACK ISBN-13: 978-0-6455221-8-1

To those who believe and participate in their faith, the pious and faithful.

Disclaimer

What is represented here is not the view of any company, organisation, group or individual other than the author's. Your interpretation of it and any consequential actions are your own.

CONTAINS RELIGIOUS REFERENCES

Table of Contents

Prologue

The depth and complexity of the words in the Old and New Testament are such that many have been unable to discern clearly their message. There are many passages written for each class in society, the farmers, soldiers, trades people, professionals and merchants. There are many layers to the truth and only God is able to know such a complex truth. Although it is my intention to write the full truth, I will undoubtedly fall short of it.

Furthermore, what was intended to be written is based on merely one perspective. Of all the layers of truth, the one that was chosen to be revealed, is the administrative cultural. This is done with regards to the State administrative systems. It is neither exclusively spiritual nor exclusively anything else, but it is part of the religion.

For a long time, people read the Bible and missed the points I will raise. They do so because they have lost understanding of the language that preserved the meaning. Also, the manipulation of the texts over the centuries has corrupted many versions. After extensive research, reading and understanding, I believe each translated Bible has been written to serve an alternative purpose.

In reviewing the manuscripts and fragments there was a disappointing and unsettling probability; those that preserved the manuscripts and fragments had most likely preserved what suited them the most. It wasn't the case where the people themselves preserved these manuscripts or fragments. It was those who had the resources and power. In addition, history tells us of times that books were burnt. But what is more sinister? Burning books or not saving them through intentional neglect. Either way we are not left with the full truth in written form.

To keep the truth, in the absence of material proof, meant we had to rely heavily on specific Church traditions. Yet the Protestant movement put faith in the written word and denounced traditions almost completely. Which without them realising, they had also taken away a substantial amount of the truth preserved as tradition. We know that the truth is the word of God, but where the word is incomplete, we must rely on traditions passed down to us. I am not taking sides in this argument beyond what I have raised. There is one Church and it is founded on the truth. Sometimes that truth relies heavily on the traditions that are kept by the people and Church.

I am the least qualified to present to you this book. All I know is that I found meanings to passages and found meaning for words I had never read in any other text. God helped to put light into my eyes. It is with piety and humbleness that I present this text, perhaps erroneous and short of perfect. I feel a fool for writing out of my area of expertise but such were the preoccupations of my thoughts at the time.

The Scriptures

This book references commonly available Biblical digital texts over the internet as a source. The two main sources are the Septuagint (the Old Testament written in Greek) and the Byzantine Majority Text (the New Testament written in Koine Greek). These texts were chosen initially because of the limitations of the author. It was possible to directly translate them with confidence. Also, the Septuagint writings are closer to what one would personally expect to be the truth of the original manuscripts. However, the invaluable value of the Masoretic texts is also noted. These assertions will become clearer in towards the end of this book.

The Septuagint

Originally, the Septuagint was copied from the Hebrew scriptures by order of one of Alexander the Great's generals, Ptolemy of Egypt. Tradition has it that 72 people translated the scriptures hence it's name and the Roman representation of it as the LXX (The Septuagint). How 72 became 70, is unknown, like all things we must be prepared to accept what is true and fix our mistakes. There is also a manuscript that exists to support the tradition, called the Letter of Aristeas. It should be noted that the number 72 is the minimum number of members that a Democratic system requires to operate, for 12 tribes. As described in the book "Democracy and the people".

The modern Septuagint often found as an internet resource is a collection of writings based on Greek manuscripts and texts. It is a

1

culmination of Manuscripts and the Codecies, Vaticanus, Sinaiticus and Alexandrinus. Where ever the majority agree that is, generally, the text used.

In addition, by simply having several surviving Greek manuscripts and fragments, these identify that there was a Biblical text written in Greek of which we call the Septuagint. Be comforted in knowing for certain that the Greek translations were authoritative and ancient in origin. Their intention at the time was to capture the full truth as close as possible to the original Hebrew manuscripts, which are now gone. We know this because it was by tradition supposed to cater for the Greek speaking population of Jews. There is affirmation that there was an Authoritative text produced in the Septuagint and New testament. Attestation for the Septuagint is achieved by the letter of Aristeas. Furthermore, a large amount of Greek inscriptions and manuscripts are being found and accordingly processed. This further highlights the importance of the Greek language towards understanding the meaning of the Bible.

The Masoretic Text

The Masoretic texts date almost a thousand years after the Greek codices (Septuagint). The oldest Hebrew texts found were the Saint Petersburg Codex, known also as the Leningrad Codex, and the Aleppo Codex. These are considered the earliest and best Masoretic texts. This is commonly known as fact, however, there was no in depth investigation and comparison of Hebrew texts while writing this.

Having the Masoretic texts as a reference when needed, proved it's value exceedingly. It was found that the Greek was a serious and reflective version of the original message in the way that it flowed. However, the Hebrew helps to clarify some parts where either the translation into Greek was not accurate or where the

Masoretic text embellishes with more detail particular passages. Both the Masoretic text and the Septuagint are invaluable.

Other Translations

Regarding the other translations; the protestants tend to use the King James Version among many. Of those translated into English, it is one of the best because of two reasons, it was printed instead of hand copied and there are minimal typographic mistakes in it. Secondly, it was copied from the existent texts for the sole purpose of preserving and attaining the most accurate translation into English. However, the Greek texts and Masoretic texts vary considerably from all the English translations, including the King James Version.

The Author corrected a bible passage 25 years ago on an online internet forum where in certain passages it would mention the words "chalice" and "goblet". The passages supposedly belonged to the KJV. A search of the KJV today found none of those phrases as were in Isaiah 51:22, not even the photographed original. This means that either the KJV removed the references to a chalice or goblet or what was quoted as being the KJV wasn't the KJV version. It could also mean that the original photographs are of a modified copy and not the original, after-all it was typed not hand written. This is why there was enormous hesitation in presenting the information contained within this text. Will what is being said be cancelled? Will it lead to more crimes against the faith and literature? Alternatively, there was a constant worry if the text referenced here was the correct text.

Also, many translations were supposed to be based on the Greek texts but I found some preferred to use the Masoretic texts combined with NT Greek. Usually relying on the Masoretic texts for the Old Testament and the Greek for the New Testament.

Ideally the texts should be quoted in Greek and Hebrew, however, this is a detailed analysis of the text and the specialisation of the Author is the Greek and Koine Greek languages. It would require many specialists to affirm what is written in the other languages. It was appropriate, therefore, to include several English translations. In this way the denominational differences would hopefully be overcome. Hopefully, any differences from the Greek would be found since there would be multiple references to the same text.

Each denomination in Protestantism uses particular version or translation. It wasn't possible to include all of them. It proved difficult to choose from all the translated bibles. However, the King James Version (KJV) and New International Version (NIV) were chosen. The NIV modernised to some degree the language of the KJV yet still conveyed the same idea. Both these Bibles are different to the Greek and Masoretic texts.

In addition, some terms found in most Bibles were most likely never used in the original bible, of which we do not have a copy of. There was a likely corruption of the text by simply keeping and preserving corrupted copies of the originals. It may not have been intentional to start with. Such as the accidental hand copied errors that would be expected. However, as time progressed even the codices and manuscripts have layers of writing on them to indicate being re-written or perhaps written over other texts.

Summary of the Codices

The original fragmented manuscripts, although reviewed, were far beyond the scope of this book and beyond my resources to assess properly. I take it in good faith that the Byzantine Majority Text and the Septuagint are a reasonable reflection of those manuscripts and fragments of papyri. I did double check, though, and found some differences. I raised some of those issues in other books, but for sake of being neutral, I refrain from identifying specific issues with the Bibles.

Despite all these aspects regarding translations, there was a need to translate directly from the Greek on numerous occasions. The existing texts of selected passages were copied into tables but this does not mean that their meanings were the same as what was written in Greek. There was no intention to translate the whole Bible, the task would be adding to the number of imperfect translations. So instead, priority was given to explain the passages in the Bible as they are understood in Greek. "No one doubts that medieval texts are often wrong. But the way to correct them is to analyse and compare them with care, not to rewrite history without them" (Treadgold, 1997).

The need for direct translation

To avoid some confusion, the following selected terms are clarified from the Greek manuscripts and fragments:

Attested Greek	Common English translation	Actual Meaning
Κύριος	Lord	The leader (Archon) of the leaders (Archons)
ἀρχόντων	Prince	The leader (Archon)… e.g. of the city.
ἄρχων	Lord	A Leader (Archon)
προσεκύνει	Worships	Bows (literally, moves forward)
Βασιλεύς	King	An Archon Magistrate; Associated with Glory, Celebrations and Events. From Christ until the middle ages it changes meaning.

Table 1. Example words given different meanings in the English translations. (Byzantine Majority Text NT, 2023; Garel & Esther, 2023; Septuagint LXX, 2023)

As an example of the type of analysis that may be undertaken in evaluating manuscripts, the following is described. The way that John 18:37-38 is read, makes more sense to say that Pontius Pilate was asking Jesus if He was the bringer of Glory or perhaps the Magistrate of Celebrations. Had Jesus claimed to be an actual King, as we know the term King, it is unlikely that Pontius Pilate would have said he finds nothing wrong with the man.

We also have some other issues where some fragments like the Ryland Papyrus P52/457, which has reconstructed text that says something slightly different to the recognised text for John 18:37. It starts off with Jesus affirming, He is the ΒΑΣΙΛΕΥΣ - Basileus (Vasileus) which gets translated as King. According to Jesus's Genealogy he has the right to claim he is a King. But instead, the term Basileus is used to say;

Ryland Papyrus P52 (RECONSTRUCTED - John 18:37-38)
ΒΑΣΙΛΕΥΣ ΕΙΜΙ ΕΓΩ ΕΙΣ ΤΟΥΤΟ **ΓΕΓΕΝΝΗΜΑΙ** ΚΑΙ (ΕΙΣ ΤΟΥΤΟ) ΕΛΗΛΥΘΑ ΕΙΣ ΤΟΝ **ΚΟΣΜΟΝ ΙΝΑ ΜΑΡΤΥΡΗΣΩ** ΤΗ ΑΛΗΘΕΙΑ ΠΑΣ Ο ΩΝ **ΕΚ ΤΗΣ ΑΛΗΘΕΙΑΣ** ΑΚΟΥΕΙ ΜΟΥ ΤΗΣ ΦΩΝΗΣ **ΛΕΓΕΙ ΑΥΤΩ** Ο ΠΙΛΑΤΟΣ ΤΙ ΕΣΤΙΝ ΑΛΗΘΕΙΑ **ΚΑΙ ΤΟΥΤΟ** ΕΙΠΩΝ ΠΑΛΙΝ ΕΞΗΛΘΕΝ ΠΡΟΣ **ΤΟΥΣ** ΙΟΥΔΑΙΟΥΣ ΚΑΙ ΛΕΓΕΙ ΑΥΤΟΙΣ ΕΓΩ ΟΥ**ΔΕΜΙ**ΑΝ ΕΥΡΙΣΚΩ ΕΝ ΑΥΤΩ ΑΙΤΙΑΝ.

(Papyri : Greek P 457, 2023; Windle, 2019)

The original papyrus is missing much of the above reconstructed text, only that in bold exists. The term ΒΑΣΙΛΕΥΣ - Basileus, for example, does NOT appear on the papyrus. If it existed it would have been on the torn part of the papyrus. Also, most of the reconstruction is derived from unknown methods and sources. However, this is where we enter what is known as the Majority Text Bibles, which use various sources and find the best fit.

Breaking down the word Basileus to root words has the following results: ΒΑΣΙ – (BASI) meaning Glory ΛΕΥΣ – (LEYS) meaning People. Where the prefix is an ancient borrowed term for Glory and the suffix is a derivative of the word for People (ΛΕΟΣ - Leos). The attested usage of the prefix in Linear B to mean some sort of fight, struggle or contest implies the word was used instead of the existing words to mean something similar to the way the military uses the term Glory. Also, if the term was borrowed from Farsi or Persian, a similar word is used to mean "Vessel" from which we get "vase" from. If it were borrowed from Persian, the phrase would have the meaning the People's

Vessel. Afterall when we say Jesus saved us, he carried all of us the same way he carried all our sins. But as time lapsed, the word simply became less impressive than what it's literal meaning was. The Basileus in the Democratic systems of Athens was a judge or magistrate selected from a pool of Archons to look after the celebrations and things associated with the Glory or Exuberance of the people. Christ came after the word had been used in this way. But later the word in the Middle Ages The Eastern Roman empire used it as a title for the emperor. The meaning changed considerably, but the literal meaning remained very similar to the People's Glory or perhaps the People's Vessel. Both make sense in the way Christ may have used the term.

In retrospect, if the reconstructed text was correct then the translation would start "Magistrate of glory am I, for this is what I was born for and for this I came…" which in our everyday language could be rephrased "The People's Glory am I, for this is what I was born for and for this I came" if Persian had been still influential at the time, "The People's Vessel am I,…" would have been stated. However, common translation of it would be "I am the King for this I was born and for this I came…" It just doesn't make sense when the common English translation is used. Hence a significant puzzlement over it's meaning. Also notice that the reconstructed Papyrus text starts off with the affirmation, not with the questioning by Pontius Pilate as used in the majority of Bibles, as follows:

Septuagint (John 18:37-38)

37 εἶπεν οὖν αὐτῷ ὁ Πιλᾶτος· οὐκοῦν βασιλεὺς εἶ σύ; ἀπεκρίθη Ἰησοῦς· σὺ λέγεις ὅτι βασιλεύς εἰμι ἐγώ. ἐγὼ εἰς τοῦτο γεγέννημαι καὶ εἰς τοῦτο ἐλήλυθα εἰς τὸν κόσμον, ἵνα μαρτυρήσω τῇ ἀληθείᾳ. πᾶς ὁ ὢν ἐκ τῆς ἀληθείας ἀκούει μου τῆς φωνῆς. 38 λέγει αὐτῷ ὁ Πιλᾶτος· τί ἐστιν ἀλήθεια; καὶ τοῦτο εἰπὼν πάλιν ἐξῆλθε πρὸς τοὺς Ἰουδαίους καὶ λέγει αὐτοῖς· ἐγὼ οὐδεμίαν αἰτίαν εὑρίσκω ἐν αὐτῷ· 39 ἔστι δὲ συνήθεια ὑμῖν ἵνα ἕνα ὑμῖν ἀπολύσω ἐν τῷ πάσχα· βούλεσθε οὖν ὑμῖν ἀπολύσω τὸν βασιλέα τῶν Ἰουδαίων;

KJV (John 18:37-38)

37 Pilate therefore said unto him, Art thou a king then? Jesus answered, Thou sayest that I am a king. To this end was I born, and for this cause came I into the world, that I should bear witness unto the truth. Every one that is of the truth heareth my voice. 38 Pilate saith unto him, What is truth? And when he had said this, he went out again unto the Jews, and saith unto them, I find in him no fault at all.

NIV (John 18:37-38)

37 "You are a king, then!" said Pilate. Jesus answered, "You say that I am a king. In fact, the reason I was born and came into the world is to testify to the truth. Everyone on the side of truth listens to me." 38 "What is truth?" retorted Pilate. With this he went out again to the Jews gathered there and said, "I find no basis for a charge against him.

Summary of the scriptures

Therefore, as stated, the complexity of determining each manuscript's interpretation and authenticity among other things is beyond the scope of this book. It's enough to say that faith should be put into the current Bibles that we use, however, we must remain diligent and alert.

With respect to the passage referencing, the numberings for the passages as found in the English translated material were preserved, so as not to confuse people. It is important to highlight that some sections in the Masoretic and Greek texts will be found in different locations to those indicated in other translated bibles. The Septuagint and Byzantine Majority Text have slightly different passage section numberings and headings to most other English translations.

The biases here, are that the purpose of this book was to focus on the cultural nature of the Biblical texts rather than any of the other aspects. The cultural aspect of particular interest are the systems of State administration. Both the Old Testament and New Testament produce interesting scenarios where many State administrative systems existed. It should be clarified that State administrative systems are the systems used to administer the powers of a city. Examples of specific types of State administrative systems include kingdoms, empires, governments and demarchic and democratic administration. This universal cultural concept of the Bible was analysed by selecting specific passages and describing the various administrative systems and determining the variables and assessing them.

To try and remain neutral excerpts from the modern Septuagint and Byzantine NT (Byzantine Majority Text), KJV and NIV were included. However, all the explanations are directly translated from the Greek. Revealing what is said in the Greek, has the intention to convey a message that is presumed lost in other

Tim Damianidis

translations. There is no intention to steer you away from which ever denominational text you use.

11

Historic scene

The scene that the Bible was set in, deserves a very brief mention. The city states and their Democratic systems were prolific in the days of the Bible's Old Testament writings. In-fact it was the rise of Alexander III, Basileus of Macedon, and his Diadochi that contributed to the end of Democracy. Then, according to the various histories, the Roman city rose and spread it's polity as an empire. It was at that time in human history that the New Testament emerged; first among the Jews and then the rest of Humanity.

2000BC - 900BC Mediterranean culture
(All the dates and date ranges are Arbitrary and only serve to help visualise the chronology of events. Under no circumstance should they be read literally.)

Approximately at the time of the collapse of the Bronze Age and the Palace economies, there was an initial spread of Democratic systems, also called Demarchic systems, throughout the world. There was a rapid Hellenic colonisation, in this time, of the Mediterranean and Asia. The rapid colonisation of the Mediterranean could have been the catalyst for culminating into what historians call the Sea People wars.

It is also the period upon which historians claim the majority of events in the Old Testament had occurred, aside the very early creation and first generations. Egyptian Biblical figures such as Ramses I and Ramses II are often referred to in this period of time. But the exact dates are unknown and could be earlier than indicated.

Also, the histories of Herodotus refers to the end of this time period. He describes that the culture of Egypt was based around being a Theocracy. Trade was occurring at significantly large levels in the Mediterranean countries with Egypt. Also, a channel was described giving the Nile economy access to the Indian Ocean (Herodotus, 2004).

The Jews were enslaved in Egypt at this time. Wandered through the desert, setup a nation and towards the end of this period there was the rule of King David.

900BC - 750BC Demarchy

The written histories of Herodotus reflect on a time starting around the fall of Troy. As a consequence, there is now archaeological and historical evidence that describes tribes organised into forms of Demarchy or perhaps Democracy. Little and sporadic evidence exists. This early period saw tribal traditions growing resembling a Democracy (Herodotus, 2004, Book III, 80) . From an archaeological point of view Ostraca or voting chips were found in numerous sites along the Mediterranean coast, Anatolia, Northern Africa and the Near East (El-din, 2023; Hawass, 2019; Millard, 1962; Youtie, 1936). The Bible, in Numbers and Judges, along with archaeological evidences highlight the traditions of using lots, sortition, ostraca (voting chips), magistrates and archons. The culture of a Democracy and the tools to operate it had been developed during the times of the Old Testament.

750BC – 359BC Democracy emerges

Then the Athenian Democracy had emerged. It was considered a
perfected system of Demarchy and hence it's name Democracy.
Pericles, one of the Archons of the Athenian Democracy had
instituted revolutionary changes. The number of participants and
the quality of the system improved through his influences.

From around Pericles's time to the time Alexander's father Philip
Of Macedon rose to power, there was a steady transition of the
Democratic system back into an Oligarchy. It was almost entirely
certain that, by the reign of Alexander III of Macedon, the
Athenians had lost a functional Democracy not just in Athens but
in almost all their colonies, league cities and imitators. The
Hellenistic period was about to begin.

Israel, Near East and Asia were being influenced into adopting
autocratic rulers modelled on Darius and his attempted
conquests. The Ionians (Greek speakers), revolted against Darius's
rule (Herodotus, 2004). It was before the rise of Darius that the
Israelites had to deal with the Assyrian, Babylonian and Persian
empires. The writings of Jeramiah in the Old testament cover the
Persian period of the Jewish people. They were captured and
brought there by their rivals. It is likely this is the period that
people had seen the difference between a Demarchy and
Kingdoms.

359 BC – 100 BC Septuagint spreads

Then between Alexander's conquests up until the Roman empire
began expanding eastward, almost every large city in the world
was under one empire. Israel, Alexandria, Syria, Anatolia, the
near East and many more places entered a Hellenistic period. The
Diadochi of Alexander, were his Generals. They took over his
empire when he fell (Arrian, 2014). Their reign caused the spread
of a common language at the time. Koine Greek became the

common language of Southern Europe, Northern Africa, The East and Asia. The Septuagint is said to have been translated in that time period. Commonly recognised is that the majority of Jews spoke Greek during that time. Hence the primary reason to have the Septuagint compiled.

100BC – 100AD Under the boot of an empire

Hellenism continued within the Roman empire. The reign of kings in the East and West, lasted from the Diadochi until modern times. To the date of writing this, we have lived without a Democracy for roughly 2400 years, the world over. Yet in between this time period came the saviour who saved us so that we could continue our faith. The birth and crucifixion of Christ occurred within a time period where Israel was ruled by Romans. Despite this rule the Israelites had their own political systems governing specific issues like religion.

With regard to the language of the Bible; Koine Greek differed from the classical or Attic Greek. We know this because a significant number of historical accounts and artifacts that place the language in that position. This is especially true for the period immediately following Alexander the Great through to the initial century after Christ of the Roman Empire. We can deduce that the population of Hellenistic Jews was exceedingly high to justify the translation of Hebrew texts to Greek.

With regards to the lost Democracy, during the reign of Alexander; Numbers, Judges and Kings represent a systematic culture change. It represents, moving through different ways of ruling and leadership. It is a story arch traversing a period that started possibly with a Democratic styled system, to an Oligarchy then the rule of Kings, to Empires and then their demise. Numbers, refers to the use of lots, or sortition, and the organisation and counting of the population. Judges refers to the hierarch magistrates that formed an Oligarchy, eg. the Levites were specific magistrates. Kings which we know as being the rule of an autocrat like David. Also, kings were considered a part of the celebrative Archons in the Athenian Democracy. They were powerless entities that were given administrative duties for city celebrations and events.

Tim Damianidis

The Messiah

It was foretold that a child would be born and will be known as Emmanuel, the God that walks with the people (Septuagint LXX, 2023, Isaiah 7:14). Emmanuel, in Hebrew, meant God among the people.

Septuagint (Isaiah 7:14)
διὰ τοῦτο δώσει Κύριος αὐτὸς ὑμῖν σημεῖον· ἰδοὺ ἡ παρθένος ἐν γαστρὶ ἕξει, καὶ τέξεται υἱόν, καὶ καλέσεις τὸ ὄνομα αὐτοῦ Ἐμμανουήλ
KJV (Isaiah 7:14)
Therefore the Lord himself shall give you a sign; Behold, a virgin shall conceive, and bear a son, and shall call his name Immanuel.
NIV (Isaiah 7:14)
Therefore the Lord himself will give you a sign: The virgin will conceive and give birth to a son, and will call him Immanuel.

The Prophecies being fulfilled

Then Micah, another prophet, foretold the birthplace of the Messiah and how he will come to power. Bethlehem would be the place that he would be born and from there the name of him will be known over the world (Septuagint LXX, 2023, Micah 5:1-3). Translating Micah 5:1-2 "2 And you Bethlehem home of the Ephratha,…" in Hebrew, meaning fruit carpous. In turn the fruit or carpous meant the Christ as used later by John (Byzantine Majority Text NT, 2023, John 15:1-8). Continuing the translation "singular against thousands of Judas, for you will be the Archon of Israel and your departure from the start will be known through the ages".

Septuagint (Micah 5:1)
ΚΑΙ σύ, Βηθλεέμ, οἶκος τοῦ Ἐφραθά, ὀλιγοστὸς εἶ τοῦ εἶναι ἐν χιλιάσιν Ἰούδα· ἐκ σοῦ μοι ἐξελεύσεται τοῦ εἶναι εἰς ἄρχοντα ἐν τῷ Ἰσραήλ, καὶ αἱ ἔξοδοι αὐτοῦ ἀπ᾽ ἀρχῆς ἐξ ἡμερῶν αἰῶνος
KJV (Micah 5:2)
But thou, Bethlehem Ephratah, though thou be little among the thousands of Judah, yet out of thee shall he come forth unto me that is to be ruler in Israel…
NIV (Micah 5:2)
But you, Bethlehem Ephrathah, though you are small among the clans of Judah, out of you will come for me one who will be ruler over Israel…

The God who walked with the people

The coming of the Christ, was important to the Old and New Testament. The Christ came among the people as one of the people. He showed us that even a God walked among the people. He didn't come on the back of an army or as a ruler of a Kingdom. The Christ showed us that even God will walk with us, the demos.

So, the birth of the Christ, the bringer of light to our lives was born in a small city known as Bethlehem. Despite being among the few he walked against thousands who had betrayed the city.

The coming of The Christ made him the true Archon (ἄρχοντα) of the people of Israel, not the ruler or lord or king. The translations are weak. He opened the eyes of those trapped in the old ways and so was known as the Archon who changed the world and He became known to the world over for ever. As prophesised by Micah (Septuagint LXX, 2023, Micah 5:2).

Archons, are a position of leadership found in a Democratic system. At the time of writing this, the deception ran deep with the term Archon. It means literally a leader that could often take the role of a magistrate but not necessarily. It did Not mean a king, ruler or monarch etc. Yet many online sources mistranslate into some kind of ruler or governor or some dominant position.

He who would walk with the people, Emmanuel, walked along side us, despite thousands opposing him. They ran to worldly wealth and spoils of war as and false idols, as described in the story of Moses and David. God remarked in paraphrase, that the will of the people shall be done. Also, it was noted that the people, that is the majority, made a choice to install an earthly King instead of having their God walk with them (Septuagint LXX, 2023, 1 Samuel 8:7).

Based on this the word God should not produce an image of a being that is above us and controlling our lives. God did not dominate us and control us, God gave us free will and freedom to be. God was before us, but God created us and came to us and will be with us till our end and beyond. These are also the foundations of a democratic view. Many argue these points and use the words of the Bible to create a picture of a Benevolent Dictatorship under God. For whatever reasons, it comforts them to view God in this way. However, it was found that the story arch, the long arch that transcends the entire Bible does not support the idea of installing a Despot or Monarch or any form of Autocrat.

Furthermore, our relationship with God is very special. Despite all of God's power, we are privileged to use that power through our work. That is, God's will, working through us. In other words, the principle here is a focus on the empowering of the people. So, our God is not a dominator, God walks with us and empowers us to do as Jesus did on Earth.

The faith would go beyond

The Israelites, would later prove to themselves that the earthly King David was of no comparison to the realm that Christ would establish. At it's zenith, the kingdom of David, like all kingdoms had finite borders and boundaries. Many speculate it reached Arabia all the way to the Euphrates river and from the Mediterranean to the start of Persia. It mattered not how big the empire was, it was limited like all of them that preceded it.

Even when God promised victories they were to show that no matter how many battles were fought and won, the limitation of an army and a state run by Oligarchs or Monarchs was never going to give what the people wanted. As an example, God in paraphrase stated that to revenge them (the Israelites) that he will send four types of things against them (Juda), the sword, dogs, beasts and birds. (Septuagint LXX, 2023, Jeremiah 15:3).

Septuagint (Jeremiah 15:3)

καὶ ἐκδικήσω ἐπ αὐτοὺς τέσσαρα εἴδη, λέγει Κύριος· τὴν μάχαιραν εἰς σφαγὴν καὶ τοὺς κύνας εἰς διασπασμὸν καὶ τὰ θηρία τῆς γῆς καὶ τὰ πετεινὰ τοῦ οὐρανοῦ εἰς βρῶσιν καὶ εἰς διαφθοράν.

KJV (Jeremiah 15:3)

And I will appoint over them four kinds, saith the Lord: the sword to slay, and the dogs to tear, and the fowls of the heaven, and the beasts of the earth, to devour and destroy.

NIV (Jeremiah 15:3)

And I will appoint over them four kinds, saith the Lord: the sword to slay, and the dogs to tear, and the fowls of the heaven, and the beasts of the earth, to devour and destroy.

In Jeremiah 15:3 the last five words in the Greek say "to-the solid and to-the corrupt". Which at first was confusing, so to add further to this, we investigate the Hebrew and there is one word between the term for sky, οὐρανοῦ, and the word for to-the, εἰς, which is Behémat. This word means, literally, something like a large beast but can mean several things such as mute or beastly or even imbecilic. Could it mean that the systems of government are the beast? Meaning all together in summary that God will revenge against the Beast (figuratively, the Government System of Juda) both the solid and corrupt in it, by sending four things against them as described. Juda at that time had raised immoral Kings whom in turn enticed their population to sin among them and against others including Israel, as described in 2 Kings (Septuagint LXX, 2023, 2 Kings 21:9-17).

Reconstructed from Greek and Hebrew (Jeremiah 15:3)
καὶ ἐκδικήσω ἐπ αὐτοὺς τέσσαρα εἴδη, λέγει Κύριος· τὴν μάχαιραν εἰς σφαγὴν καὶ τοὺς κύνας εἰς διασπασμὸν καὶ τὰ θηρία τῆς γῆς καὶ τὰ πετεινὰ τοῦ οὐρανοῦ, [Behémat] εἰς βρῶσιν καὶ εἰς διαφθοράν.

By combining the Hebrew and Greek we get a significantly different meaning as pointed out, one that makes sense. Rather than translate the entire passage the meaning now changes in the passage by including the end phrases that were removed from the English translations because they probably didn't make clear sense without reading directly from the Greek and using the Hebrew only as support as done here.

God helping doesn't mean he agreed

Retrospectively, the original argument is that despite the support of God during the entire Bible, the purpose of that support was not always to purely gain a victory, but also to teach a lesson. Although specific to the Islamic borders with Christianity, and despite disagreeing with many of his opinions, Kaldelis raises a few arguments that are transferrable. "Borders exist if (and only if) a state authority has the ability to intervene and regulate or restrict that movement. That is what a border is, and there is every indication that for most of its long history the Roman state had the infrastructural capability to operate them to its advantage" (Kaldellis, 2023). This was certainly true of the Roman empire, most of the time. However, the statement is universally true, in that even during the establishment of Jerusalem, regarding the location and boundary of the twelve tribes, the borders were finite zones as pointed out in Ezekiel (Septuagint LXX, 2023, Ezekiel 48:1-7).

It makes things clear to us that even when God was supporting the Israelites he wasn't doing it because of his own will alone, but the will of the people. In this way God helped the Israelites considerably and showed them that without God they would not get as far as they did. The will of the people can be seen as a Democratic principle. At the same time the long arch of the story shows us that even with this help the word or truth is limited to travel to the kingdoms' or empires' boundaries and not much beyond. Together with what we read in the Old and New Testaments, it makes it clear that, in contrast, Christ and the Apostles would deliver the light, as prophesised, to the entire world.

The bloodlines he denounced

In retrospect the Apostles wrote about the birth experience also. But the texts, we have, begin with a justification of bloodlines between Abraham, King David and Jesus (Byzantine Majority Text NT, 2023, Mathew 1:1-17). At first it may seem a paradox to begin with a bloodline genealogy, unless it was to highlight the fact that Jesus rejected any and every title and claim to the rule of Israel. It would be likened to having a choice to join the ranks of those that rule and instead choosing to walk among the people in a Democratic cultural fashion.

Then it was proclaimed by the Apostles that the prophets did foretell that the saviour would be born to a virgin, and that the child would be male and given the name Emmanuel, to mean God among the people (Byzantine Majority Text NT, 2023, Mathew 1:18-25). Joseph, knowing the prophecy, called Emmanuel the Saviour (Isous in Greek). Hence how we know Emmanuel as Jesus (Isous).

Now, some will argue with what has been written, it has not been written in this way before. But there is hope to make what is said as clear as possible. It is this Saviour or Messiah, who took the brunt of the persecution of the ideal he stood for. He personified not only God but also walked among us a man. He saved us by dying so that we may preach the word and continue the ideal and the idea and the dream and the reality and the foundation upon which everything depends on. He died for us, so that we all may continue the faith and live. But what was in our faith all this time? I believe it had been layered in such a way that there was something in it for everyone. But there is also a niche meaning to it that revolves consistently around the concept of Democracy.

The God who healed

To make the bias of this writing clear and having said the previous, the healing of Jesus was an important part of the faith too. Jesus did not confront the unjust and smite them. Instead, he healed those in most need and especially those with the greatest faith. As we are told by the evangelists, Jesus cured a man of leprosy (Byzantine Majority Text NT, 2023, Mathew 8:1-4, Mark 1:40-45, Luke 5:12-14). Therefore, what is said about the administrative systems and culture of the people should be taken as a supplement to the vast depth of the scriptures.

In the passage from Mathew 8:1-4, Mark 1:40-45, Luke 5:12-14 it should be stated that Jesus was not seeking worship. Yet the words begged, worship and prostrated are used to describe the Leper's actions when approaching Jesus. The Greek uses the word most similar to prostrated but not implying to the ground but a tilted bow to show respect. When Darius III was defeated and died, Alexander was sole ruler of the Achaemenid Empire. He introduced proskynesis based on the customs of the Persians (Arrian, 2014, 4.10.5). The type of Proskynesis or bowing was not clear. However, only slaves would typically touch their knees to the ground. In most archaeological depictions it appears that a bow was offered in respect of the Autocrat by citizens. However, slaves and servants would be required to further touch their knees to the ground. Perhaps in this instance the proskynesis was low and appeared to be worshipping or begging as the Evangelists point out.

BMT (Mathew 8:1-4) see also Mark 1:40-45, Luke 5:12-14

Η΄\ΚΑΤΑΒΑΝΤΙ δὲ αὐτῷ ἀπὸ τοῦ ὄρους ἠκολούθησαν αὐτῷ ὄχλοι πολλοί. 2 Καὶ ἰδοὺ λεπρὸς ἐλθὼν προσεκύνει αὐτῷ λέγων· Κύριε, ἐὰν θέλῃς, δύνασαί με καθαρίσαι. 3 καὶ ἐκτείνας τὴν χεῖρα ἥψατο αὐτοῦ ὁ Ἰησοῦς λέγων· θέλω, καθαρίσθητι. καὶ εὐθέως ἐκαθαρίσθη αὐτοῦ ἡ λέπρα. 4 καὶ λέγει αὐτῷ ὁ Ἰησοῦς· ὅρα μηδενὶ εἴπῃς, ἀλλὰ ὕπαγε σεαυτὸν δεῖξον τῷ ἱερεῖ καὶ προσένεγκε τὸ δῶρον ὃ προσέταξε Μωσῆς εἰς μαρτύριον αὐτοῖς.

KJV (Mathew 8:1-4)

8 When he was come down from the mountain, great multitudes followed him. 2 And, behold, there came a leper and worshipped him, saying, Lord, if thou wilt, thou canst make me clean. 3 And Jesus put forth his hand, and touched him, saying, I will; be thou clean. And immediately his leprosy was cleansed. 4 And Jesus saith unto him, See thou tell no man; but go thy way, shew thyself to the priest, and offer the gift that Moses commanded, for a testimony unto them

NIV (Mathew 8:1-4)

8 When Jesus came down from the mountainside, large crowds followed him. 2 A man with leprosy came and knelt before him and said, "Lord, if you are willing, you can make me clean." 3 Jesus reached out his hand and touched the man. "I am willing," he said. "Be clean!" Immediately he was cleansed of his leprosy. 4 Then Jesus said to him, "See that you don't tell anyone. But go, show yourself to the priest and offer the gift Moses commanded, as a testimony to them."

This is our Jesus, the one that was prophesised, the one that walked with us. Who taught us and healed us. The one who despite being of imperial house, chose the realm of the people. Our saviour was wise and knowing of many ways. This is among the many reasons we glorify God, Christ and the Holy spirit.

Tim Damianidis

Heavenly Plans

There will not be a condemnation then or now of those who are working with Jesus. Not in terms of physical flesh but in terms of the spirit (Byzantine Majority Text NT, 2023, Romans 8:1). As already noted, this meant that those who follow Christ will be saved spiritually as they will live a life free of burdens and sins. Culturally speaking, the suffering of Christ enshrined and preserved his testament so that future generations would not suffer the same way. We are already saved.

If we are saved, then what are the plans for us from this point forward? The best way to describe the next step is to refer to Romans 8:14-17 which reads that we are heirs to God and co-heirs to Christ (Byzantine Majority Text NT, 2023, 8:14-17). Some argue that this may mean we are Gods or become Gods, but that is not the case. We are children of God. Jesus told us that we can essentially do anything he does, as he spoke to the Apostles (Byzantine Majority Text NT, 2023, John 14:12). All this together tells us that we are destined to walk together with Christ on Earth, spiritually, and inherit with Christ what was created for us.

Working with God makes us Heirs

BMT (Romans 8:14-17)
14 Ὅσοι γὰρ Πνεύματι Θεοῦ ἄγονται, οὗτοί εἰσιν υἱοὶ Θεοῦ. 15 οὐ γὰρ ἐλάβετε Πνεῦμα δουλείας πάλιν εἰς φόβον, ἀλλ᾽ ἐλάβετε Πνεῦμα υἱοθεσίας, ἐν ᾧ κράζομεν· ἀββᾶ ὁ πατήρ. 16 αὐτὸ τὸ Πνεῦμα συμμαρτυρεῖ τῷ πνεύματι ἡμῶν ὅτι ἐσμὲν τέκνα Θεοῦ. 17 εἰ δὲ τέκνα, καὶ κληρονόμοι, κληρονόμοι μὲν Θεοῦ, συγκληρονόμοι δὲ Χριστοῦ, εἴπερ συμπάσχομεν ἵνα καὶ συνδοξασθῶμεν.

KJV (Romans 8:14-17)
14 For as many as are led by the Spirit of God, they are the sons of God. 15 For ye have not received the spirit of bondage again to fear; but ye have received the Spirit of adoption, whereby we cry, Abba, Father. 16 The Spirit itself beareth witness with our spirit, that we are the children of God: 17 And if children, then heirs; heirs of God, and joint-heirs with Christ; if so be that we suffer with him, that we may be also glorified together.

NIV (Romans 8:14-17)
14 For those who are led by the Spirit of God are the children of God. 15 The Spirit you received does not make you slaves, so that you live in fear again; rather, the Spirit you received brought about your adoption to sonship. And by him we cry, "Abba, Father." 16 The Spirit himself testifies with our spirit that we are God's children. 17 Now if we are children, then we are heirs—heirs of God and co-heirs with Christ, if indeed we share in his sufferings in order that we may also share in his glory.

By receiving the spirit we are free of the bondage and fear. We are told that we too are children of God. We are further told that we are true heirs of God and the co heirs with the Christ (Byzantine Majority Text NT, 2023, Romans 8:14-17). What is the Spirit? The message or word delivered to us. It is what unites us all with God and Christ.

The word God can take several meanings. The word for God, Theos as used in the Bible can mean the magistrate or judge or most important position. Hence the "The-"derived from Thesis or position and "-os" meaning an emasculative "of". "Of the position" this is it's literal meaning but many translated the word "position" as throne and therefore God was imagined on a throne. But this is not the reality. It can also mean a spiritual position by a spiritual entity. Therefore, it has in classical Greek and later Koine Greek several meanings. When God described to Moses what to call him,

God and our memory

Septuagint (Exodus 3:14)
καὶ εἶπεν ὁ Θεὸς πρὸς Μωυσῆν λέγων· ἐγώ εἰμι ὁ ὤν, καὶ εἶπεν· οὕτως ἐρεῖς τοῖς υἱοῖς Ἰσραήλ· ὁ ὢν ἀπέσταλκέ με πρὸς ὑμᾶς
KJV (Exodus 3:14)
And God said unto Moses, I Am That I Am: and he said, Thus shalt thou say unto the children of Israel, I Am hath sent me unto you.
NIV (Exodus 3:14)
God said to Moses, "I am who I am. This is what you are to say to the Israelites: 'I am has sent me to you.'"

The word for God further is often translated "I am that I am" but there is a loss of meaning in such translation. God said I am The ὤν (On). The Greek word ὤν, could mean the entity. So, this phrase we know well, it could be saying "I am the entity". In loose translations it could also be "I am that is" In English it's translations give the impression that God is part of Creation as a being "I am". But a Being is not the nature of God from our texts. God is "the entity that is", this is what the scriptures say. Now where and how God exists is most likely not within the Creation but beyond it and unknown to us. If God was a part of Creation, as a being within it, then God would be limited by the Creation.

In retrospect this also affirms that as heirs it does not mean that we will become Gods or sit on a throne or have some type of physical kingdom. It means we will take a position or thesis spiritually alongside Christ and act in the stead of our God while living. That is to say, God's will and the spirit will work through us. In Romans 8:17 it further states that if we suffer together in unity with Christ and God, then we will also be glorified together (Byzantine Majority Text NT, 2023, Romans 8:17). This is most likely expressed in the tradition of saying "αιωνία η μνήμη" - "Eternal be thy name" over the dead at a funeral. So that we glorify Christ and the fallen together.

Lessons of the Oligarchy and Monarchy

Isiah says that God has a plan and that everything that was planned for, will be fulfilled (Septuagint LXX, 2023, Isaiah 14:24). It is made clear that those on the correct path will know it because God will watch over them, instruct them and even counsel with them (Septuagint LXX, 2023, Psalms 32:8). As an example of how God's will was done, the section of the Bible called Numbers begins with Moses taking a register of citizens and hence a list of fighters (Septuagint LXX, 2023, Numbers 1:2).

Septuagint (Numbers 1:2)
λάβετε ἀρχὴν πάσης συναγωγῆς υἱῶν Ισραηλ κατὰ συγγενείας αὐτῶν κατ᾽ οἴκους πατριῶν αὐτῶν κατὰ ἀριθμὸν ἐξ ὀνόματος αὐτῶν κατὰ κεφαλὴν αὐτῶν πᾶς ἄρσην
KJV (Numbers 1:2)
Take ye the sum of all the congregation of the children of Israel, after their families, by the house of their fathers, with the number of their names, every male by their polls;
NIV (Numbers 1:2)
Take a census of the whole Israelite community by their clans and families, listing every man by name, one by one

Under the commands of Moses twelve tribes were united with a Democratic manner. We know this to be a Democratic way, because Aristotle describes the same system for Athens (Aristotle, 2013). But Levi was given the task to protect the tabernacle which was the holy place housing the scriptures and other items (Septuagint LXX, 2023, Numbers 1:47-54). It was a plan that Moses wrote as being inspired by God. Therefore, what was said by God was done.

Septuagint (Numbers 1:47-50)

47 οἱ δὲ Λευῖται ἐκ τῆς φυλῆς πατριᾶς αὐτῶν οὐκ ἐπεσκέπησαν ἐν τοῖς υἱοῖς Ἰσραηλ 48 καὶ ἐλάλησεν κύριος πρὸς Μωυσῆν λέγων 49 ὅρα τὴν φυλὴν τὴν Λευι οὐ συνεπισκέψῃ καὶ τὸν ἀριθμὸν αὐτῶν οὐ λήμψῃ ἐν μέσῳ τῶν υἱῶν Ἰσραηλ 50 καὶ σὺ ἐπίστησον τοὺς Λευίτας ἐπὶ τὴν σκηνὴν τοῦ μαρτυρίου καὶ ἐπὶ πάντα τὰ σκεύη αὐτῆς καὶ ἐπὶ πάντα ὅσα ἐστὶν ἐν αὐτῇ αὐτοὶ ἀροῦσιν τὴν σκηνὴν καὶ πάντα τὰ σκεύη αὐτῆς καὶ αὐτοὶ λειτουργήσουσιν ἐν αὐτῇ καὶ κύκλῳ τῆς σκηνῆς παρεμβαλοῦσιν

KJV (Numbers 1:47-50)

47 But the Levites after the tribe of their fathers were not numbered among them. 48 For the Lord had spoken unto Moses, saying, 49 Only thou shalt not number the tribe of Levi, neither take the sum of them among the children of Israel: 50 But thou shalt appoint the Levites over the tabernacle of testimony, and over all the vessels thereof, and over all things that belong to it: they shall bear the tabernacle, and all the vessels thereof; and they shall minister unto it, and shall encamp round about the tabernacle.

NIV (Numbers 1:47-50)

47 The ancestral tribe of the Levites, however, was not counted along with the others. 48 The Lord had said to Moses: 49 "You must not count the tribe of Levi or include them in the census of the other Israelites. 50 Instead, appoint the Levites to be in charge of the tabernacle of the covenant law — over all its furnishings and everything belonging to it. They are to carry the tabernacle and all its furnishings; they are to take care of it and encamp around it.

It's hard to tell the exact system and dates used because there is a lack of specific documentation. The Greek version of the administrative state system that became known as the Democracy existed for thousands of years but was only documented for a short period of time some say between 500 and 359BC (the commonly known date of Philip Of Macedon and later Alexander the Great's Rise).

It should also be stated that there are elements of the Democratic system predating it and living beyond those dates. Therefore, the balances and checks of the Democratic system were God's intervention through randomised sortition (Numbers), and using that method to appoint temporary magistrates (Judges). However, almost every system mentioned in the Bible: A Theocracy (Septuagint LXX, 2023, 1 Samuel 12:12), Oligarchy (Septuagint LXX, 2023, Numbers 1:47-50) and Monarchy (Septuagint LXX, 2023, 1 Samuel 8:22) etc almost entirely omit the description of a Democracy. Yet all of the components of a Democratic system were described.

In addition, and to clarify, the word Democracy is used because the word Demarchy is a specific word with different meaning today. By categorising by the number of leaders it should be correctly called from most to least Demarchy, Oligarchy and Monarchy. Instead, we use the word Democracy to infer a state of power held by the people. But in the case of the Old Testament one of the problems faced was that people kept resorting to false paths and idols in life; dead ends. They worshipped the wrong things and expected miracles from the wrong entities. Also, they failed to take power of the state and operate and administer their own affairs. In doing so, their hands were not working the will of God.

Before these events involving Moses, the book of Judges states
how there was no king at the time that the events in Judges were
about to occur, and that each person did what they believed was
in their eyes correct (Septuagint LXX, 2023, Judges 21:25).

Septuagint (Judges 21:25)
ἐν ταῖς ἡμέραις ἐκείναις οὐκ ἦν βασιλεὺς ἐν Ισραηλ ἀνὴρ ἕκαστος τὸ εὐθὲς ἐν ὀφθαλμοῖς αὐτοῦ ἐποίει
KJV (Judges 21:25)
In those days there was no king in Israel: every man did that which was right in his own eyes.
NIV (Judges 21:25)
In those days Israel had no king; everyone did as they saw fit.

Having a permanent magistrate group looking over the
Tabernacle gave Levi exceptional political and religious power
hence establishing a Theocratic state. It wasn't seen by Moses but
he had given Levi an Oligarchical position under a Theocratic
state. This was necessary in the long arch of the story, as
Democracies or similar free systems are not very good at
mobilising for war. Simply because they delay the process
significantly because of the consultative process. Although,
leagues of city states can respond quickly, they had a tendency to
fight city by city against the same opponent as described by
Thucydides (Thucydides, 2013). God's plan as it was worked
through others served several purposes not just the immediate
needs of the people calling for change. It was served to them also
as a lesson not as a gift.

But in saying this we must draw attention to the statement in
Samuel. Where the Lord spoke to Samuel and told him, listen to

the people's voice and install a king (Septuagint LXX, 2023, 1 Samuel 8:22).

BMT (1 Samuel 8:22)
καὶ εἶπεν κύριος πρὸς Σαμουηλ ἄκουε τῆς φωνῆς αὐτῶν καὶ βασίλευσον αὐτοῖς βασιλέα καὶ εἶπεν Σαμουηλ πρὸς ἄνδρας Ισραηλ ἀποτρεχέτω ἕκαστος εἰς τὴν πόλιν αὐτοῦ
KJV (1 Samuel 8:22)
And the Lord said to Samuel, Hearken unto their voice, and make them a king. And Samuel said unto the men of Israel, Go ye every man unto his city.
NIV (1 Samuel 8:22)
The Lord answered, "Listen to them and give them a king".

So, you see that they started with a liberal system without a name or specific type, yet most likely some form of Democracy (Septuagint LXX, 2023, Judges 21:25). Then they created what was almost a Democratic system with sortition and magistrate roles etc. however, it was a Theocratic Oligarchy established by Moses (Septuagint LXX, 2023, Numbers 1:47-54). Then finally, it led to a Monarchy being elected by the people's voice (Septuagint LXX, 2023, 1 Samuel 8:22). On the last point it was an ironic twist, to have God listen to the voice of the people, whom in His wisdom knew they were making a mistake.

Then it was the Levites that came to judge Jesus much later in the story of the Bible. Along with the Levites came the Jerusalem priests, as stated by John (Byzantine Majority Text NT, 2023, John 1:19). They came as permanent magistrates, Hierarchs of an Oligarchical Theocratic system not only to see who Jesus was, but to judge his words.

BMT (John 1:19)
Καὶ αὕτη ἐστὶν ἡ μαρτυρία τοῦ Ἰωάννου, ὅτε ἀπέστειλαν οἱ Ἰουδαῖοι ἐξ Ἱεροσολύμων ἱερεῖς καὶ Λευΐτας ἵνα ἐρωτήσωσιν αὐτόν, Σὺ τίς εἶ;
KJV (John 1:19)
And this is the record of John, when the Jews sent priests and Levites from Jerusalem to ask him, Who art thou?
NIV (John 1:19)
Now this was John's testimony when the Jewish leaders in Jerusalem sent priests and Levites to ask him who he was.

The long arch of the story transcends the entire bible and in that the truth of what was being said can be understood. There was no perfect administrative system of the people. But certain systems had qualities that were of need at the time. To prove to us that an Oligarchy was the most fearsome and harshest of the systems, it was the Hierarchs, the Levites, that ultimately judged an innocent man.

Genesis 11:4 talks of creating a city by the people and for the people with a tower in the heavens (Septuagint LXX, 2023, Genesis 11:4). Meaning a system by the people and for the people to abide by the ethics of our God before we spread the system and faith to all parts of the world. As already discussed elsewhere the people in those days did as they wanted.

Babel was a gift

Septuagint (Genesis 11:4)
καὶ εἶπαν δεῦτε οἰκοδομήσωμεν ἑαυτοῖς πόλιν καὶ πύργον οὗ ἡ κεφαλὴ ἔσται ἕως τοῦ οὐρανοῦ καὶ ποιήσωμεν ἑαυτοῖς ὄνομα πρὸ τοῦ διασπαρῆναι ἐπὶ προσώπου πάσης τῆς γῆς
KJV (Genesis 11:4)
And they said, Go to, let us build us a city and a tower, whose top may reach unto heaven; and let us make us a name, lest we be scattered abroad upon the face of the whole earth.
NIV (Genesis 11:4)
Then they said, "Come, let us build ourselves a city, with a tower that reaches to the heavens, so that we may make a name for ourselves; otherwise we will be scattered over the face of the whole earth."

This passage proposes that Democracy and the faith were supposed to spread on the back of the people not an empire. To clarify, there was an intention to establish a city for the people and by the people ie a democratic state. They also wanted to build a tower which has symbolic meaning as described later. Then they intended to spread everywhere across the globe. God was impressed with what they had done yet there was also great concern. A significant translation issue are the terms πρὸ τοῦ which translated to "lest we" in the KJV and "otherwise" in the NIV. The correct translation should be "before". In changing this simple phrase the entire meaning of the situation is changed. There was an intent to build a model city upon which all other

40

cities would be based upon and to spread that model across the Earth.

Septuagint (Genesis 11:5-7)
5 καὶ κατέβη Κύριος ἰδεῖν τὴν πόλιν καὶ τὸν πύργον, ὃν ᾠκοδόμησαν οἱ υἱοὶ τῶν ἀνθρώπων. 6 καὶ εἶπε Κύριος· ἰδοὺ γένος ἓν καὶ χεῖλος ἓν πάντων, καὶ τοῦτο ἤρξαντο ποιῆσαι, καὶ νῦν οὐκ ἐκλείψει ἀπ᾽ αὐτῶν πάντα, ὅσα ἂν ἐπιθῶνται ποιεῖν. 7 δεῦτε καὶ καταβάντες συγχέωμεν αὐτῶν ἐκεῖ τὴν γλῶσσαν, ἵνα μὴ ἀκούσωσιν ἕκαστος τὴν φωνὴν τοῦ πλησίον.
KJV (Genesis 11:5-7)
5 And the Lord came down to see the city and the tower, which the children of men builded. 6 And the Lord said, Behold, the people is one, and they have all one language; and this they begin to do: and now nothing will be restrained from them, which they have imagined to do. 7 Go to, let us go down, and there confound their language, that they may not understand one another's speech.
NIV (Genesis 11:5-7)
5 But the Lord came down to see the city and the tower the people were building. 6 The Lord said, "If as one people speaking the same language they have begun to do this, then nothing they plan to do will be impossible for them. 7 Come, let us go down and confuse their language so they will not understand each other."

God wanted them to spread all over the Earth but not as one united empire. The tower represents a double-edged sword. On one side of the blade, the tower represented their faith and how they wanted to worship God. Then the other side of the blade was seeking for selfish glory through imperial actions. In both instances God did not want to be glorified by towers or for humanity to live within an empire.

With respect to the translations, having seen that humanity was capable of achieving anything they set their minds to, God is said to have separated them by language and distance. So, they were spread out as a league of separate states divided by many languages and they were sent to settle separate parts of the world. It was made difficult for them to unite as one empire with one language. This identifies that even God from the Old Testament wanted humanity to live freely and not united in an empirical fashion. Not just then, but also today, this message should be acknowledged. It is further stated in unquoted text that the city and tower where no longer commissioned.

Could it be that cities come second to tribes? Were we expected perpetually to live tribally? Afterall the city and tower representing an empire were left unattended. This clearly states that the existence and power of the tribes must permeate through the system being developed. This is also the foundation of the Democratic state. Whereby, we are given the idea that united tribes are permissible, but a city that gives no voice to the tribes is as described in Genesis, an abomination.

God of the living, act while you can

Before making a final conclusion, the next step is to assess what is written in the New Testament. It appears that the same plan was revealed in the Old and New Testament, in the way that the plan was not to have God as our dominator. Nor was it to establish a Theocracy, Oligarchy or Monarchy. In-fact they were used as examples that they were not the answer as exemplified by the story of the entire Bible. Also, God partook alongside us as described earlier. But more importantly as Christ spoke according to Mathew, that to love God, with all your heart, spirit and mind is first and to love those by our side like ourselves is second (Byzantine Majority Text NT, 2023, Mathew 22:37-40). Meaning that loving of the people and Christ by our side implies all those with the same love of God. It is as if the first and second point are the same but priority is given to God. Our citizenship therefore is defined by our faith and love in God and Jesus and one another. We do not have a physical kingdom waiting for us, instead we have an obligation to establish a state system of administration that is powered by the people of faith for the people of faith. This is the conclusion of the very early writings of our faith. Because it is not the afterlife to which we must wait for, but this living world that we must work in.

BMT (Luke 20:38)
Θεὸς δὲ οὐκ ἔστι νεκρῶν, ἀλλὰ ζώντων· πάντες γὰρ αὐτῷ ζῶσιν.
KJV (Luke 20:38)
For he is not a God of the dead, but of the living: for all live unto him.
NIV (Luke 20:38)
He is not the God of the dead, but of the living, for to him all are alive."

So you see, we must work for the long arch to be established, while we are living. But God never says install a Democracy. Yet, we are given all the tools and knowledge to implement one. We are given hints that perhaps it is the system that will exist when the pious inherit the Earth. But before concluding this, it is important to realise that it was all planned from the start. Also, that everything in between was to show that nothing is perfect. Finally, without us first seeking to be better as individuals no matter which system is in place, it will be become corrupt. Hence the teachings of Christ.

The Teachings

The failed commune

The teachings of the apostles demonstrate that they also
attempted different systems. They tried Communism or some
variation of it throughout the part known as the Acts of the
Apostles. It also failed. In Acts 4:32-37 It describes how the wealth
of the participants as much as almost everything material else was
shared in a commune (Byzantine Majority Text NT, 2023, Acts
4:32-37).

However, it should also be pointed out that material wealth and
assets are ultimately controlled by the state. In a Democratic
society that would mean that the entire treasury of the state was
in the hands of the citizens. In this case what was shared was also
controlled by those that controlled the wealth and currency. The
authority of the commune was headed by a higher authority also
known as an oligarchy.

This is specifically an example of communism, but it is also a trait
found in those establishing a democratic commune. However, in
this case it was traditionally acknowledged that the system was a
Christian commune. It also proved that, so long as Oligarchs
control the system, there is no escape. Often people will highlight
it was the way for the future, however, they ended up packing up

the commune.

BMT (Acts 4:32)
Τοῦ δὲ πλήθους τῶν πιστευσάντων ἦν ἡ καρδία καὶ ἡ ψυχὴ μία· καὶ οὐδὲ εἷς τι τῶν ὑπαρχόντων αὐτῶν ἔλεγεν ἴδιον εἶναι, ἀλλ᾽ ἦν αὐτοῖς ἅπαντα κοινά.
KJV (Acts 4:32)
And the multitude of them that believed were of one heart and of one soul: neither said any of them that ought of the things which he possessed was his own; but they had all things common.
NIV (Acts 4:32)
All the believers were one in heart and mind. No one claimed that any of their possessions was their own, but they shared everything they had.

At the time preceding and immediately after the stoning of Stephen the commune existed and many prayed for courage. It also caused the leaders of the commune to disperse to different locations. Be it the will of God or a result of the ongoing Christian persecution is unknown. Acts 5:17-41 certainly highlights there was a persecution of the Apostles, it is highly likely it continued after Stephen's death. Also, although the Bible does not stipulate clearly what happened afterwards to the commune, the participants did leave Jerusalem to fulfil their duties elsewhere (Byzantine Majority Text NT, 2023, Acts 7:54).

For many reasons including the traditionally established arguments between Greek speaking Jews and Hebrews, the hierarchy of the church needed to change. As mentioned in the Acts: some were better at spreading the word and others better at setting tables. Although they solved the situation with another Oligarchy, by electing seven deacons, this it's self later contributed to the demise of the commune. The election of the seven (Byzantine Majority Text NT, 2023, Acts 6:1-7) appeased the people but it doesn't say that it was for the benefit of the united church. You see at every turn where someone in the Bible had to make a decision they tried to solve things by installing Oligarchies or people in charge. These eventually corroded and worked against the church. Had none of them stood above anyone else and shared the burden as it was foretold, they would not have had Stephen resort to delivering powerful speeches and standing out tall among the rest. But it was Stephen who in Christ's example spoke and then forgave those that killed him and was Martyred so as to end the commune (Byzantine Majority Text NT, 2023, Acts 7:54-60).

While many systems were discussed in the Bible, the only system that was kept till last, was the system for the meek. Jesus according to Mathew stated that the believers or pious will inherit the earth (Byzantine Majority Text NT, 2023, Mathew 5:5). In other words, the citizenship will be the pious and the reward a city among many that belong to the people.

BMT (Mathew 5:5)
Μακάριοι οἱ πραεῖς: ὅτι αὐτοὶ κληρονομήσουσιν τὴν γῆν.
KJV (Mathew 5:5)
Blessed are the meek: for they shall inherit the earth.
NIV (Mathew 5:5)
Blessed are the meek, for they will inherit the earth.

In conjunction with the previous, in my book "Democracy and the people", I list specific quality based attributes needed in a Democratic system, points a to h.

a. Participation

The democratic principle of participation is supported by the words of the Apostle Mark. Not only did Jesus walk among us he came to serve too and not only that but to give his life to save others (Byzantine Majority Text NT, 2023, Mark 10:45).

BMT (Mark 10:45)
Καὶ γὰρ ὁ υἱὸς τοῦ ἀνθρώπου οὐκ ἦλθεν διακονηθῆναι, ἀλλὰ διακονῆσαι, καὶ δοῦναι τὴν ψυχὴν αὐτοῦ λύτρον ἀντὶ πολλῶν.
KJV (Mark 10:45)
For even the Son of man came not to be ministered unto, but to minister, and to give his life a ransom for many.
NIV (Mark 10:45)
For even the Son of Man did not come to be served, but to serve, and to give his life as a ransom for many.

This is a duty to serve the church and people. However, in democratic systems the church or general assembly has a prerequisite of participation, just like the spiritual church. It requires serving the people as Christ did.

b. Invest all our time into the Work

Later when a person asked Jesus to come in and rest Jesus responded that he had work to do. I must do holy work now that there is an opportunity to because night will come and we won't have the power to work (Byzantine Majority Text NT, 2023, John 9:4).

BMT (John 9:4)
4 Ἐμὲ δεῖ ἐργάζεσθαι τὰ ἔργα τοῦ πέμψαντός με ἕως ἡμέρα ἐστίν· ἔρχεται νύξ, ὅτε οὐδεὶς δύναται ἐργάζεσθαι.
KJV (John 9:4)
I must work the works of him that sent me, while it is day: the night cometh, when no man can work.
NIV (John 9:4)
As long as it is day, we must do the works of him who sent me. Night is coming, when no one can work.

That is to say totalitarian or harsh times (night) will come and it will stop people from being able to perform even the most basic duties. To say this, He knew what would come after his death. As we already mentioned some parts of the persecutions continued into our modern age.

In terms of an administrative system, this means that there will be times when an ideology will not be able to be expressed because of the oppression or suppression it faces. It means that in a Democratic manner everyone has the same burden, and everyone needs to carry some part of it. Otherwise, the ideology fails. As I said before, there are spiritual things we are overlooking. You see if we all believed in the good and learned the ways that Jesus showed, we would not need an administrative system to operate our state. But it is assumed we need it because we are weak in our faith, holistically.

c. The more we put it the better it is

BMT (Galatians 6:4-5)
4 τὸ δὲ ἔργον ἑαυτοῦ δοκιμαζέτω ἕκαστος, καὶ τότε εἰς ἑαυτὸν μόνον τὸ καύχημα ἕξει, καὶ οὐκ εἰς τὸν ἕτερον. 5 Ἕκαστος γὰρ τὸ ἴδιον φορτίον βαστάσει.
KJV (Galatians 6:4-5)
4 But let every man prove his own work, and then shall he have rejoicing in himself alone, and not in another. 5 For every man shall bear his own burden.
NIV (Galatians 6:4-5)
4 Each one should test their own actions. Then they can take pride in themselves alone, without comparing themselves to someone else, 5 for each one should carry their own load.

The work is for everyone to achieve and as such does not need to be justified to anyone, everyone carries as much of the same burden as they can (Byzantine Majority Text NT, 2023, Galatians 6:4-5). It is not only saying that you must work as a team it is saying that we must try to take equal burden so we don't justify any boasting but rather get on with the job. The job being working to realise the plans established side by side with God.

d. Juries

Points a. to c. have been covered but the issue of juries, point d., is somewhat vague in the Bible. The term for jury, enorkoi (ἔνορκοι), meaning those sworn in, does not appear in many places in the Bible (that I could find) . The Jury and it's operation are not covered very well in the Bible. However, one passage stands out of the twenty odd similar statements:

Septuagint (Nehemiah 6:18)
ὅτι πολλοὶ ἐν Ἰούδᾳ ἔνορκοι ἦσαν αὐτῷ, ὅτι γαμβρὸς ἦν τοῦ Σεχενία υἱοῦ Ἡραέ, καὶ Ἰωνὰν υἱὸς αὐτοῦ ἔλαβε τὴν θυγατέρα Μεσουλὰμ υἱοῦ Βαραχία εἰς γυναῖκα.
KJV (Nehemiah 6:18)
For there were many in Judah [sworn unto him], because he was the son in law of Shechaniah the son of Arah; and his son Johanan had taken the daughter of Meshullam the son of Berechiah.
NIV (Nehemiah 6:18)
For many in Judah were [under oath] to him, since he was son-in-law to Shekaniah son of Arah, and his son Jehohanan had married the daughter of Meshullam son of Berekiah.

Note: The parts in braces in both Greek and Hebrew have the meaning Jurists meaning from Latin those sworn into service.

It is likely that there was a form of jury used in the administrative systems used during the times of the Old Testament. It is likely as in this example to have become related to the way the Church operated it's religious affairs. In-fact, the system of Athenian Democracy had yet to be established, during the early times of the

Old Testament, but by the time the New Testament was written the Democracy was trapped under the boot of the Roman empire.

In addition, the fundamental working mechanisms for Juries and other systems were in place. As mentioned, the Israelites had something similar to Democratic systems but they were corrupted slowly over generations. They had sortition systems, voting, elections, judges, archons, and all the fundamental components of a Democracy. They just never throughout the Old Testament or New Testament had an opportunity to express it as an administrative system. We get a rough idea that some kind of Demarchy existed (Judges 21:25). While a substantial amount of the bible relates to not judging as individuals, there is ample advice on how to judge as part of a jury, if you have to. Further highlighting that judges and juries existed.

Given the prerequisites of a Democratic system; that the people have the power to operate their Legislature, Judiciary and Enforcement, it then comes down to, how? While the complete answer is not mentioned in the Bible, we have other sources of information that guide us to the belief that juries were not so much fairer but were necessary to fulfil the ideology that the people operate all facets of their state administration. To inherit the earth, they would need to inherit administration over their own affairs also.

Also, this does not mean almost all other aspects of a Democracy were not established. For example, random Sortition was described clearly:

e. Lots and f. sortition

BMT (Acts 1:26)
Καὶ ἔδωκαν κλήρους αὐτῶν, καὶ ἔπεσεν ὁ κλῆρος ἐπὶ Ματθίαν, καὶ συγκατεψηφίσθη μετὰ τῶν ἔνδεκα ἀποστόλων.
KJV (Acts 1:26)
And they gave forth their lots; and the lot fell upon Matthias; and he was numbered with the eleven apostles.
NIV (Acts 1:26)
Then they cast lots, and the lot fell to Matthias; so he was added to the eleven apostles.

When the time came to replace Judas the Apostles prayed and cast lots and the "cleros" or lot fell to Matthias and as such he was numbered after the 11 apostles (Byzantine Majority Text NT, 2023, Acts 1:26).

This further high-lights, that despite the crushed Demcoratic city states. The underlying ethos and customs of a Democratic system continued into the era of the New Testament, despite the persecution and obstacles to it's operation, Israel had documented in the Bible a continuation of Democratic principles. So, regarding points f. and g. randomisation was present and it allowed for God's intervention in decisions. Then finally judges and magistrates were appointed from the pool of Archons to perform specific duties. Unlike the Athenian model, the Israelite model tended to consistently appoint people in charge or leadership in doing so tended to form Oligarchies and Autocracies.

Septuagint (Leviticus 19:15)
Οὐ ποιήσετε ἄδικον ἐν κρίσει· οὐ λήψῃ πρόσωπον πτωχοῦ, οὐδὲ μὴ θαυμάσῃς πρόσωπον δυνάστου· ἐν δικαιοσύνῃ κρινεῖς τὸν πλησίον σου.
KJV (Leviticus 19:15)
Ye shall do no unrighteousness in judgment: thou shalt not respect the person of the poor, nor honor the person of the mighty: but in righteousness shalt thou judge thy neighbour.
NIV (Leviticus 19:15)
'Do not pervert justice; do not show partiality to the poor or favoritism to the great, but judge your neighbor fairly.

On the issue of point f. There are several passages regarding the issue of judging. It is phrased in a way that some interpret to mean the casual judgment of others in day to day life. But for it to be given such emphasis and the way it is phrased, implies that there were juries in Israel, as there were in other cities. Given the evidence of ostraca in Israel, among other artifacts, there is in conjunction with Biblical texts enough to assume that Juries existed and are attested.

g. Fair Juries and Judges

BMT (Mathew 7:1-2)
1 ΜΗ κρίνετε, ἵνα μὴ κριθῆτε· 2 ἐν ᾧ γὰρ κρίματι κρίνετε κριθήσεσθε, καὶ ἐν ᾧ μέτρῳ μετρεῖτε μετρηθήσεται ὑμῖν
KJV (Mathew 7:1-2)
1 Judge not, that ye be not judged. 2 For with what judgment ye judge, ye shall be judged: and with what measure ye mete, it shall be measured to you again.
NIV (Mathew 7:1-2)
1 Do not judge, or you too will be judged. 2 For in the same way you judge others, you will be judged, and with the measure you use, it will be measured to you.

To this point it has been established that almost all the points raised, with respect to determining the quality of the Democratic state, have been satisfactorily addressed in the Bible. However, there is the issue of Ethics, point h. That is the final point raised in the list provided.

Ethics are the most important aspect when running a Democratic state. Without ethics and some restraint the entire system can collapse into a corrupt Ochlos or Pleistocracy. I do not want to write a complete book on ethics here. However, the subject is enormous. From my work in occupational health and safety, came these Biblically attested virtues or desired ethics.

h. Ethics

Virtues	Effects
Courage	Impacts participation. By encouraging people, the participation grows.
Justice	Ensures fair treatment to issues and cases. Fair elections, voting and decision making. Honest and transparent systems.
Truthfulness	Accurate information.
Fortitude	To persevere with work that is required.
Diligence	To ensure fair elections and processes.
Temperance	To share experience and knowledge. To inform, consult and cooperate in a mannered way.
Patience	To give change management time to take effect.
Kindness	To ensure trust and ongoing sharing of information, cooperation and consultation.
Humility	A leader isn't always a hero, most of the time leadership requires an emotive connection to a person and the catalyst is usually humility.
Respect	To cooperate and consult with others

Table 1 Democratic virtues affirmed by the Bible.

However, in addition to all this, improvement of our ethics begins with the self.

BMT (Mathew 7:5)
ὑποκριτά, ἔκβαλε πρῶτον τὴν δοκὸν ἐκ τοῦ ὀφθαλμοῦ σου, καὶ τότε διαβλέψεις ἐκβαλεῖν τὸ κάρφος ἐκ τοῦ ὀφθαλμοῦ τοῦ ἀδελφοῦ σου.
KJV (Mathew 7:5)
Thou hypocrite, first cast out the beam out of thine own eye; and then shalt thou see clearly to cast out the mote out of thy brother's eye
NIV (Mathew 7:5)
You hypocrite, first take the plank out of your own eye, and then you will see clearly to remove the speck from your brother's eye.

Therefore, we have a serious task ahead of us. We are not asked to unite under one empire. We are asked to unite city by city and spread the word so that we may all live in peace and harmony, love and respect for each other.

Our Stand

In summary, our God walked among us to show us that even if the temptation to rule, dominate or govern others is offered to us, we should never accept. We must walk in the pathway of Christ because we too are children of God and we will inherit the earth. God, Christ and the Holy Spirit are the God of the living, not the dead. What we do in our life is what is judged not thereafter. So, given that, under the guidance of God, we have tried every other system known to us and it has failed, we are left with one system yet to try, Ethical Democracy.

In the Old and New Testament, the plan seems to be one that describes the features of a Democracy reoccurring. In saying this there is no head of state, we are all heirs and rightful occupants of the Democratic state because we are all children to the same ethical entity we know as God. Our purpose is to teach these things and grow in numbers so that we may bring the prophecies to light, by working the will of God through our bare hands.

To the church and it's citizens

The example of Christ needs to reverberate throughout the Church he established. He did not pour concrete and call it foundations, he built the Church upon the actions of the Apostles. Just like we today build with our very actions the Church from within. So must those in the Church return to the Democratic ways shown to us by Jesus and the Apostles. The ways of the sortition allowing God to influence the outcome, randomisation of duties, temporary seats of administrative power and so forth. The church must again lay the foundations upon our shoulders.

Also, while Christs bloodlines were recorded so that they served the purpose of demonstrating what he renounced. But what purpose does an Apostolic bloodline serve? To prove the same or the opposite? Where is your statement to renounce rightful rule in place of walking among the people of the church? That is the starting place, not a division within, but an assertion of what is our faith and what is not our faith. Dispense the traditions of Autocratic rule and dominance. Our God was not that. We are brothers and sisters in a family that should work together. When the Church restores itself to the Church that Christ lay foundations for, is when the second coming will be possible.

Once the leaders of our church have understood the mistakes of the past, they may guide the church into a new future that it's self may take a long time to achieve, piece by piece. I hope for patience and unity this time around. We do not want another schism to add to the existent 40,000 denominations. The three largest should consider, at least, unity through a Democratic league. Not an attempt to dominate or underpin each other and force ones' dogma on another. The entire future of humanity rests with the direction that the Church takes, inclusive of all denominations.

To all the people

As for the rest of humanity, there is a clear indication that our God demanded citizenship through a common faith. But it was made clear that such unity should never be through an empire or a sprawl of cities. If people, for example, all believe in a Democracy, then they can function as citizens in a city. However,

60

believing in something else means the faith is different and often incompatible. The same can be said of our faith in the entity that is, God. Some will believe in the Tri hypostatic nature of God, while others will not. Some will seek the truth elsewhere. None of those other faiths provide the same passive expectation to love thy neighbour, to such an extent so as to do their will over our own. Love goes beyond mere tolerance; love implies a person can listen to another's debate and decide appropriately on a case or matter.

How can a Democracy exist at the same time as a Monarchy or Oligarchy? The Hybrid systems that use a little of each system can exist, but they are not effective at delivering any of the virtues a person would expect from their State administrative system. It is better that each to their own than trying to all be one thing. Better there be several churches so long as within each one is a common faith. The league is still possible, but what good is a neighbour who does not love you back? These are hurdles that must be overcome if any brotherhood is to be expressed between all people.

The God of Christianity, is likely the same as others. The differences in each faith are that God used the Holy Spirit to deliver, either, a different Message to these people or the original message was distorted. Perhaps it was to show us that what we aspire to has already been tried, perhaps it was necessary for that specific time. Is all this relevant now? What do we do with the way we are now? Do we have to be paranoid like the birds of prey of being someone's meal? Or do we take faith truly to heart and accept all humanity for what they are?

The Godly plan never intended for all of us to unite under one leader, empire and language, we established this in the story of Babel, Genesis 11:4. We as humans want to keep our tribes and our customs and our ways. But who said we can't form a league of tribal cities instead of nations? City by city, living free in a Democratic league? Each one with it's own ways and customs.

We as humans have done everything we can to create the perfect system of State administration. However, the one system not elaborated on was when Jesus Christ our God walked with us. He did so in a system similar to a school of thought and as a teacher. Similar to the Buddhist schools that developed. As already stated, that system led to Jesus's crucifixion. We the Soldati, Soldiers and Hoplites, even the Crusaders and Mujahideen are all to blame too, in blindness we not only crucified Jesus we then warred with each other senselessly for millenniums. Such is the corruption of the people, they crucified their own God. Does that not say it all? The Bible shows us, that even God walking among us will never work as a State administrative system. If you see it in this way you can understand that the perfect system doesn't exist. It relies entirely on how good we are as people and individuals. This is why Jesus set out to set the word straight for all of us not just one part of the world.

Even the forgotten Democracy was tried and it failed before the events of the New Testament. Where it survived, in the not so well documented Old Testament times, people had become so evil that it was pointed out that Sodom and Gamora were destroyed by God. But of all the systems we had and have the one that allows us to unite freely and transparently, the one that does so with peace and love, is Democracy.

So then to conclude, the religious institutes have a task to bring us closer together, by first fixing what is wrong within. Those things will be between the leaders to discuss initially, but eventually the league of institutions must include the faithful as leaders in their own right. The people must return to the Church and the Church must be the people with their God. To do this requires the people to begin understanding the task ahead. Teaching what needs to be taught and sharing the idea again. Nothing new has been said, it was there from the beginning. We the people need to begin first with ourselves, ensuring we are awake and ready to work for the task ahead.

Harmony and Love

The true Oligarchs, those who control the affairs of many cities, must listen to the reasons why we have come to this point. There is room for a King, Basileus and an Elder and many magistrates and Archons in the system I have described. It is merely the balance of powers that must every now and then be challenged.

We all want to peacefully graduate into a system where everyone has respect for each other. Not one class over another. Not one family or clan over another. To be fair, we want to live in tranquillity and enjoy our abilities from one another so much as they enhance our lives. This is the beauty of the people.

Yet we need to fix a significant amount of ourselves. We need to take action and show our numbers so that we are respected and never trodden over by the very laws that govern over us again. We turn to God to bless us with harmony and love for all including those that have trespassed against us and those who continue to do so. It is through that love that even those above us will learn to show their love too.

As prophesised, Christ will come again, but this time we must pave the way properly. We must not judge unfairly those with authority, we must not enrage them, yet we must work diligently with the purpose of learning the full truth. We must leave all the distractions aside to do this.

All the systems of state administration have failed. Without us working to be better as a people and a church we will never find a solution. If we are prepared then change will come through love and respect for our work. This is why we were instructed to teach the Truth with Love, by our God. Love must exist for all, including our Monarchs, Kings, Oligarchs and Archons. Love thy neighbour and thy enemy.

BMT (Mathew 5:43:45)

43 Ἠκούσατε ὅτι ἐρρέθη, ἀγαπήσεις τὸν πλησίον σου καὶ μισήσεις τὸν ἐχθρόν σου. 44 Ἐγὼ δὲ λέγω ὑμῖν, ἀγαπᾶτε τοὺς ἐχθροὺς ὑμῶν, εὐλογεῖτε τοὺς καταρωμένους ὑμᾶς, καλῶς ποιεῖτε τοῖς μισοῦσιν ὑμᾶς καὶ προσεύχεσθε ὑπὲρ τῶν ἐπηρεαζόντων ὑμᾶς καὶ διωκόντων ὑμᾶς. 45 ὅπως γένησθε υἱοὶ τοῦ πατρὸς ὑμῶν τοῦ ἐν οὐρανοῖς, ὅτι τὸν ἥλιον αὐτοῦ ἀνατέλλει ἐπὶ πονηροὺς καὶ ἀγαθοὺς καὶ βρέχει ἐπὶ δικαίους καὶ ἀδίκους.

KJV (Mathew 5:43:45)

43 Ye have heard that it hath been said, Thou shalt love thy neighbour, and hate thine enemy. 44 But I say unto you, Love your enemies, bless them that curse you, do good to them that hate you, and pray for them which despitefully use you, and persecute you; 45 That ye may be the children of your Father which is in heaven: for he maketh his sun to rise on the evil and on the good, and sendeth rain on the just and on the unjust.

NIV (Mathew 5:43:45)

43 "You have heard that it was said, 'Love your neighbor and hate your enemy.' 44 But I tell you, love your enemies and pray for those who persecute you, 45 that you may be children of your Father in heaven. He causes his sun to rise on the evil and the good, and sends rain on the righteous and the unrighteous.

References

Aristotle. (2013). The Complete Works of Aristotle (E. M. Edghill, Trans.). In: Delphi Classics,.

Arrian. (2014). The Anabasis of Alexander (E. J. Chinnock, Trans.). In. London.

Byzantine Majority Text NT. (2023). Byzantine Majority Text NT. In. Constantinople: Patriarchate of Constantinople.

El-din, s. w. (2023). Unpublished Demotic Ostraca. مجلة كلية الاداب.جامعة المنصورة.
https://www.academia.edu/87081403/Unpublished_Demotic_Ostraca

Garel, A. B. h., & Esther. (2023). Ten Coptic Ostraca at the IFAO. *Bulletin de l'Institut français d'archéologie orientale*(119), 51-77.
https://www.academia.edu/94303212/Ten_Coptic_Ostraca_at_the_IFAO

Hawass, Z. (2019). Ostraca: From the Valley of the Kings. *1*.

Herodotus. (2004). The Histories (G. C. McCaulay, Donald Lateiner, Trans.). In: Barnes & Noble Classics.

Kaldellis, A. (2023). *Byzantine borders were state artifacts, not "fluid zones of interaction"* (D. G. Tor & A. D. Beihammer, Eds.). Edinburgh University Press. (The Islamic-Byzantine Border in History: From the Rise of Islam to the End of the Crusades)

Millard, A. R. (1962). Recently Discovered Hebrew Inscriptions. *Tyndale Bulletin, 11*.
https://doi.org/https://doi.org/10.53751/001c.32351

Papyri : Greek P 457. (2023).
https://www.digitalcollections.manchester.ac.uk/view/MS-GREEK-P-00457/2

Septuagint LXX. (2023). Septuagint LXX. In (based on Manuscripts, Vaticanus, Sinaiticus, Alexandrinus ed.). Constantinople: Patriarchate of Constantinople.

Thucydides. (2013). The Complete Works of Thucydides (B. Jowett, Trans.). In: Delphi Classics,.

Treadgold, W. (1997). Review of Whittow, Making of Orthodox Byzantium. *International History Review*.

Windle, B. (2019). The Earliest New Testament Manuscripts. https://biblearchaeologyreport.com/2019/02/15/the-earliest-new-testament-manuscripts/

Youtie, H. C. (1936). Ostraca from Sbeiṭah. *American Journal of Archaeology*, *40*(4), 452-459. https://doi.org/10.2307/498797

About the author

Tim Damianidis is a business person and family man with connections around the world. He has a Graduate Diploma in Occupational Health and Safety and has worked in numerous businesses.

www.ingramcontent.com/pod-product-compliance
Lightning Source LLC
Chambersburg PA
CBHW070011100426
42741CB00012B/3200